Primal Sketches

# Primal Sketches

Caroline  Wong

Clarise Foster, Editor

EDITIONS

Cover design by Doowah Design.
Photo of Caroline Wong by Leonard Wong.

This book was printed on Ancient Forest Friendly paper.
Printed and bound in Canada by Hignell Book Printing.

We acknowledge the support of The Canada Council for the Arts and the Manitoba Arts Council for our publishing program.

Library and Archives Canada Cataloguing in Publication

Title: Primal sketches / Caroline Wong ; Clarise Foster, editor.
Names: Wong, Caroline, 1942- author. | Foster, Clarise, 1955- editor.
Description: Poems.
Identifiers: Canadiana 20210137029 | ISBN 9781773240862 (softcover)
Classification: LCC PS8645.O458 P75 2021 | DDC C811/.6—dc23

Signature Editions
P.O. Box 206, RPO Corydon, Winnipeg, Manitoba, R3M 3S7
www.signature-editions.com

*For*

*Leonard, Wesley, Eric and Calvin*

*My parents: Wah Chee Lum and Nuey Yong Lee*

# Contents

# 1

## Living at the Edge

# 2

## The Animals That Serve Us

# 3

## What Runs in My Veins

# 4

## Unmarked Paths

# 5

## The Way Home

# 1

## Living at the Edge

Yangtze

*Morning*

from the door of her old home she watched
the river daily rise. Most of the people

*Leaving*

forced out of their village
the century-old town.

*Bai Di among the clouds*

They fled carrying tools, beds, tables, chairs
to the hastily built new town
with no place for raising ducks and chickens.

*Jiang Ling a thousand li east*

At night she dreamed of water
rising over the threshold

carrying out her bloated corpse,

*gibbons from red cliffs*
*their ceaseless howling*

floating along with carcasses
of pig, cow, deer, and other debris

*while sampan lightly sailed*

down the river through the vanishing gorges

*ten thousand peaks.*[1]

---

[1] Lines in italics indicate a poem by Li Po (701–762 CE), "Morning Leaving
Bai Di Cheng," the author's translation.

## Toxic Waters

Driven from his village home by the killing river
the threat of forced termination

he, his wife, daughter and unborn son lived on discarded
plastic collected at the edge of the new town.

He tried to grow onions and spinach
in a patch of dirt around a utility pole

but the municipal police came
trampled the vegetables and hauled him away.

# Bones and Seeds

*— after Thomas Heise* (Horror Vacui)

My birthright I have exchanged for an alphabet
tablet and a dirge. I have pawned my Confucian
ink stone for an amber the colour of unpreserved bones.

If I could sail on an ox bladder on a vertical
ocean I would burn my nostalgia to honour
the cinnamon peeler in the moon.

For some of us, home is a leprosy
we carry throughout our journey west
bereaved of Monkey's eight-fold tests.

I sleep today. My mother, long dead, cracks open
her sarcophagus to make room. "Ma, I'm not ready yet."
In answer she bestows upon me three blessings.

The sun beams seeds of incandescent catastrophe.
A stick girl plants flamingos in a broken lawn.
It's no one's birthday. Some stars are not yet born.

## Battered

The purple black eye you wear, a Remembrance poppy.
The crack in your bones the lifeline across your palm you raise

to shield against Category Five disasters: Andrew
Mitch, Katrina, Missouri floods, Sudan droughts.

Makeshift shelters and refugee camps a haven
but your physically inferior body is never safe.

As always, force a legitimate form of panacea
for their self-justifying grievances.

It's your hands that go on to restore whole forests.
Heal the decrepit, the permanently disabled and wounded.

Yet you continue to rebuild your house with straw and sticks.
When you go into the woods, you wear your black hooded dress.

It turns into a scarlet, gold-hearted hibiscus
that opens in the morning and quickly dies in the night.

# Hero

When the drums and bombs stop beating and falling
and the men sit down at conferences to talk peace

it's time for you to take cover under your mother's wings.
Not the feathery wings that wrap you tightly

when you try to sleep while shreds of fallen towns
and villages rain down like flaming confetti.

You want her wings to be a shield of iron when your combat-
fatigued father comes home changed

brings home with him unhealed wounds
and the deadly tactics of war that made him a decorated hero

but your mother's papery wings burst
into flames the moment you both turn to flee.

# Apparatus

*— for Ann Jones: War Is Not Over When It's Over*

There are doors people kept closed
to block out the cries and screams of desperation
but she opened hers wide

gave the women in our village cameras
to record our daily lives

living under our men's rules.

Through the apparatus's sharply focused eye
we slowly saw the darkness
that ground our bodies down like meat

our eyes blinded
our calloused hands and feet tied

tongues cut
like those of our mothers
grandmothers, great-grandmothers.

We were not even good enough
to eat dirt.

From the array of our photographs
we saw for the first time
the daily battles we fought
to survive, feed our children.

From the scars in our throats
words began to bubble.

For the first time in our lives
we dared to open a crack
the door that locked us in.

## A Village Drama

Shrill curses volleyed between her harsh breaths
her look murderous, her hair like rags
her bruised yellow face soot-caked, tear-streaked,

the shrieking girl she dragged by her thin arms
and thrashed against the haystack
as though her small body a rice stalk.

Yet we stood and watched
as though the revolutionary army opera troupe
had come to the village square

rehearsing a new propaganda
in which the starving mother
kills to spare her daughter's unwanted life.

## Lotus Girl

Half out of the sky, the gibbous moon
floats between branches of dogwood.

No chance for the stars to break through.
Clouds and grass a rain-stitched

carpet on which to fly straight into the pool
of drowned longing.

Rise, my lotus girl, who sits shy and sweet
fecund with Pablo's leaves.

Plug your ears against the courtier's serenades
bled now of concretized lies and heat.

Go where a stranger's touch, his wordless pleading
will not move you

where the one worthy of your heartbreak
pens:
> *The green grass in the meadows*
> *Grows long with your absent shadow.*

## Two Women in the Desert

The thin old woman who carries a bundle of twigs
on top her head peers up
at the huge billboard at the edge of the village
where the desert creeps closer every year.

The young woman in the air-brushed ad—
her dark hair cascades, her cheeks round
her lips full and softly rouged
her bare arms and shoulders strong and firm.
Her whitened skin glows.

The old woman, her bony, sun-cracked face
a nest of deep lines, her body bent,
has been up since daybreak and walked for hours
along the dried-up river
where small trees, shrubs and grass
used to grow, to search for scraps of firewood.

She can't read the words along the bottom
of the billboard. Her childhood spent
helping her mother work the patch of arid land,
later caring for her through debilitating illness
and then death brought on by overwork,
malnourishment, disease.

She is held by the young woman's assured gaze.
But as the light shifts, she sees a young girl
peering from the darkness behind her door
and is blinded by the expanse of marching sand
                            the devastating storm at its wake.

# Kasbah

The advancing desert is creeping closer
toward the newly constructed gates
the crush of mud brick dwellings beyond,

tinted rose grey under the bright sun
rising one above the other—

You can almost hear again the cacophony
of flutes and tambourines playing

gaggles of hawkers and caravan traders
shouting and haggling up and down

narrow, crowded alleys and lanes
where street dancers, puppeteers and fortune-

tellers beckon, each with their own craft of magic
the air thick with dust, smoke, perfumes, spices.

Beggars and thieves jostled among richly attired patrons.
Urchins wove in and out of throng of donkeys, horses, camels
wild with anticipation.

Now, through the gates
the guides in their royal blue costumes

lead herds of eager tourists, undeterred historians
television documentarians, movie makers—

who stroll past crumbled walls
careful of broken steps as they climb.

Thread their way up and down narrow lanes
                                        empty of voices.

Peer into windowless rooms

bereft of bejewelled crystals
silk carpets, opulent tapestries purveyed

by distant traders who once stopped here
on long treks across vast seas and continents.

Their world subject even then
to countless cycles of obliteration
and light.

# 2

# The Animals That Serve Us

## Initiation

Blood spurted
from where the cleaver had slid
as distant temple gongs reverberated.

In the frantic struggle between
her clutching hand and instinct
the chicken broke free, running around and around
its plucked throat half hinged,
trailing a crimson stream across the bricks.

At the last moment her hand had relented
as she thought of the dog taking off
at the sight of the men, the rope.

The chase had lasted mere minutes.
When they reached open ground
they'd swiftly swung the rope, the dog
over the waiting post.

She had fallen, watching
hitting the stool between her legs.
She had bled. So much blood,
adrenaline pumping through her veins.

# Idylls

On the narrow dike between quilted green paddies, a boy riding a
buffalo plays his flute. Notations of musical notes somersault like flock of
swallows from his lips.

The two ducks go through the same evening ritual waddling back from
foraging fields. Up and down the lane one would walk the other home;
then vice versa, until the women come out to separate them for the night.

The New Year piglet, pampered and fatted all year in its pen, is now ready
for market.

The goose too, though it was kept all year in a narrow-necked cistern.

They say rats skinned, pressed, cured and dried are a delicacy, and in time
of drought and starvation, a life-saving food source.

Under a yellow-hazed sky, the defeated farmer, back bent by the hard
ground, the obdurate plow, repeatedly whips his hired, contumacious ox.

The ox's mournful bellowing all night. At dawn, the thin, sharpened knife
falters in the farmer's hand at the huge drops of its tears before he acts,
catching with a chipped enamelled basin the warm, iron-rich jets pulsing
from its neck.

## Bears of Yan An

Forty to fifty in one pit the baby black bears
sprawl on rusty platforms.
The ones with no place to lie down
pace around the concrete wall
careful not to step on fecal mounds.

The adolescent bears have an exercise staircase
they endlessly climb. Others stand with heads raised
in anticipation, mistaking the tourists for their keepers
who appear twice daily with pails
enriched to boost the bears' bile-producing capacity.

The adult bears are kept next to the near-airtight
processing and marketing hall flooded in cold fluorescence.
Long pampered, the bears' gall bladders balloon
with thick green liquid. They move slowly
well suited for the gowned and masked herbalist

who strokes their soft bellies with one hand
and with the other inserts a syringe fitted with a long needle.
The bears with no more bile to give are let loose in woods
and hills they have never known.

Daily they wander in shrinking circles in search
of the concrete perimeter, their human keepers.

# Tapping Animals in the Wild

Plastic collars are a nuisance
but better than to be shot dead
with a vengeance.

There are other indignities
loathsome inconveniences
painful impositions.

You could be trapped
chased, captured, anesthetized
branded, tattooed, tagged
monitored, tracked
fitted with shock collars
radios, subcutaneous chips
your ears and toes clipped at birth

all to keep animal traffickers
and global poachers
from snaring, chaining, hacking,
skinning, stripping, snipping
your organs, limbs
for fashion apparels
purses, shoes
ashtrays, tabletops, lamps
or exclusive items on menus
exotic pets.

## View from Below: Farmed Fish

No fear of us finned citizens staging an uprising
marching up the shore into your towns and cities
in our scale-plated armours and mails.

Although we are not wholly happy with our conditions
or with the governments who leave the business of
aquaculture in the hands of corporate entrepreneurs
we are naturally shy and peaceful creatures.

We lack political clout and training.
Media coverage is sometimes sensational
sometimes sporadic, depending on their notion of
newsworthy news. Others who fervently voice
their outrage and concerns, calling for our rights,
tend to move on to other issues of the day.

Those discontented come from only a small segment
of our population. The majority of us are satisfied.
We have medicare. Antibiotics are freely dispensed.
Our medical facilities are not crowded or reserved only
for the wealthy.

We are encouraged to have numerous offspring,
although there's a problem with overcrowding.
Our societal structure is communal.
Our meals are balanced and served on time.
The food enriched with vitamins and supplements
regulated with care. We love large social gatherings.
For recreation we can swim to our hearts' content.
Also deep diving.

We have no worries about our kids' schooling.
Their future is guaranteed. This easy living is spoiling me.
Mortality is no longer what it used to be.
My muscles are flabby, my eyes filmy.

Mucus tends to clog my throat and lungs.
The only other complaints I have are the prevalent
tail nipping and biting, the chronic lice infestation.
But what can we expect, living in such a closed net community.

## Case of a Pet Cow without Papers

It was not the farmer's intention to disregard
government rules and regulations
or cause trouble for anyone.
His boy had grown fond of the young cow,
running down to the pasture
after his lessons to feed and pet her
grazing with the herd.

The father had refrained from the process
of registration, health inspection
for his son's pet, and branding.
The latter had always troubled him,
not only of the pain it caused, the lingering
suffering afterwards. It reminded him of the days
of slave masters who had to chain
and mark their property as proof of ownership
making them less human.

The district agent on his annual inspection
discovered his own oversight
and took the cow away.
The father was summoned to court.
The judge, after a brief deliberation
delivered his carefully thought-out verdict.
To set an example he labelled the unauthorized
unauthenticated, and unidentified cow
an "illegal alien," a potential threat.

He sentenced her to be incinerated
along with other suspects
and fined the father 1000 euros.[2]

---

[2] From *Issues in Green Criminology: Confronting harms against environments, humanity and other animals.* Edited by Piers Beirne and Nigel South. Cullompton, Devon, UK; Portland, Oregon, USA: Willan Publishing, 2007.

# APHIS[3]

It was his job as inspector to scrutinize
analyze, weigh the apparent harms
to the test subjects
against the greater benefits to humans.

As he worked on his final reports
he thought of the numerous research labs
he'd inspected, funded by the government
pharmaceutical manufacturers, the military
where the animals varying in size, weight, species
were blinded, their eyelids sutured shut or removed
subjected to corrosive chemicals, thermal burns
radiation, electric shock, mostly through the feet or tail
sleep deprivation, extreme cold or heat
biological and chemical weapons, lasers
high-power microwaves.

When he submitted
his final assessments and conclusions
he was pricked by a nagging need
to go out to look for less stressful employment
which shouldn't be difficult
given his string of college degrees.

---

[3] USDA's Animal and Plant Health Inspection Service

## Pig as Objet d'Art

You are forever at our service
routing out gourmet truffles
sometimes guarding our perimeters
keener than our dogs.

Barbecued, roasted
sautéed, fried, stewed
smoked, cured
you come graciously
to our tables.

Entertain us in storybooks
bedtime stories
comic strips
*Looney Tunes*
*Disney* films.

Now you have risen even higher
in our esteem
with your skin tattooed and painted
in multicoloured designs and patterns
intricate, dramatic

a living art, adored, celebrated
auctioned, collected, displayed
                              long after.

## Still Life: Donkey

Left here by its owner
the donkey waits in the middle of the empty parking lot
as the sun climbs the distant ridge.

As the day heats up
and the cool desert wind stops blowing
there is no escape for it
                no defence
against the swarms of hungry black flies
from boring into the open sores on its back
except to shift a leg now and then,
or swing its head at them
            but it's no use.
As soon as it stands still again
            they are back feasting.

Seeming inured to the burning sun
it will remain standing here all day
unflinching and obedient
                as though chained.

# Unconditioned

*—for our cat, Spooky (1998–2016)*

Push of a plunger
promise of a thousand-gossamer sleep—

The light of countless gifted days
held in an infinitesimal moment
in your golden gaze
                                    let go.

No secret cave into which you hid
no soothing hand
no magic herbs
no tender potions

nothing
had helped to mitigate.

Had there been an instinctual glimmer
a primal inkling—
Vanished with your final eye blink.

At home
we gather up your things:
a worn sock
a gnawed stick
water dish...

Everything reminds.

# 3

## What Runs in My Veins

## What We Carry

Immigrants.
Exiles.
Sojourners.
Refugees.

Dunes in the desert.
Petals torn in a storm.

Useless the stars to guide us.
The gods, silent.

There are missing pages of history.
Stories told from father to son.
Mother to daughter.

We can turn the corner of unconsciousness
unravel the dreams of unsleep

but we have only what we carry:
wounds that never heal
scars left by lack and aggression
a thirst for reason and sanity

memory of lost homes.

## Where We Land

Propelled by the pull of corpuscles
desire, coded chains
the unreliability of space
the drumbeats of those
yet born, ancestry—
where our weighted ships land
is only an accidental hiatus
in our search for geography.

No one can tell you where our voyage begins.

Not in the milling stars
the precarious seas.
Nor in the centuries sculptured on cliffs
the rivers' unsteady courses.

In the countless profane reasons
held sacred to cheat our sense of direction
unknown cartography
yet to be drawn
by those who walk on, barefoot.

## Master of Nets

I am intruding upon the Master of Nets' garden, disturbing old ghosts hovering above half-hidden moongates. Narrow paths wind past rock mountains. Carved dragons in white-marble flight. Sweeping eave pagodas rise from waxy lotus pads and mallard ducks....

Endless corridors carry me to shadow-filled mansions, their faded vermilion doors half open, held by loose hinges and corroded chains. Inside: dust floats in semi-darkness. In the air, mildew of the century dead: the poster beds, the pear wood chairs, the empty shelves where once books of bamboo, the blank walls on which silk scrolls had hung, their flowering pine stumps and mist-shrouded crags....

Standing on the threshold I am reluctant to take leave. A part of me lives in the floating dust, in the footfalls gathering in the dusk....

## Miracles

Random, sleight of hand?—
a single spark
light
seed
where it falls.

Science or faith?—

From our human desire
the need to perpetuate our name
arises a whole population of fragile beings.

That we are standing here—
testimony to generations
of undefeated dreams and conquests
struggles and perseverance

pulled by the same unseen power
given to all things that live.

## Enduring Will

Fragile beings:
Cut       our flesh bleeds
Fall       our bones break.

Our bodies humbled
by fatal diseases and infections
heartbreaks, hysterical fits
mental breakdowns, dementia.

Our mortality threatened
by natural and human disasters
caused by floods, fires, volcanoes
tidal waves, hurricanes, drought
deforestation, erosion, hunger
internecine wars, genocides, rebellions
power-crazed anarchy, greed
accidents, murders, additives
illicit drugs, deluded leaders
outdated laws, worn beliefs.

Yet you and I have come through
the pernicious centuries
a double-helical twist
driven by an unstoppable imperative
a will to endure, carry on.

## Magic/Realism

Hummingbird windmills
sonic boom at subatomic range, zeroing in.

Somewhere in the Himalayas a rock loosens.
A climber misses a step, curses.

Minuscule whirlwind barely disturbs the mass
of tubular-mouthed fuchsia drooping in the aftermath

of a drenching September rainfall.
Days have passed since the last time I ventured

out except to harvest the last of string beans, fuzzy
squashes, half-ripe tomatoes, split, green sap oozing

nutrients for ubiquitous fruit flies, wasps
bumblebees, half drunk, clumsy.

Down by the lake I miss the geese
that have taken early flights

south, driven by unseasoned cold.
Three families I watched last summer

raising broods so large in number I feared
how the parents could ever care for them

keep them all safe. My heart broke each time
I tallied the slowly fledging goslings, dwindling...

Chorus of distant honking, closing in.
My autumn mood lifts at the perfect V

of their onward flight, arrowing
a miracle in perseverance and number.

## The River Heals

Beside the river
the rumble of canning machines ceased.
Fleets of seiners and gillnetters gone.

Where the old wharf once stood
grey pilings like fossil bones
bask in the mid-August sun.

In the heritage museum an incongruous collection:
nets, floats, old ledgers, leftover cans, boning knives

along with ghost village
of empty buildings and houses
once built for company managers,
foremen, net loft bosses, accountants.

The Skeena flows on, unhurried and clear.
In its mirror of inverted sky, mountains, trees
I imagine seeing the teeming salmon returning
to spawn in upstream beds.

Crows caw.
Above the woods an eagle circles.
At the shore's edge, a heron poises on one leg, waits...

In our absence the river heals
its fragile calm watched by ring of mountains
balanced between nature and our greed.

## Dawn: Inner Mongolia

The moon follows and lights my steps
through stub grass
purple corona weeds
goat droppings.

In the distance
warriors in their silk armours
ride bareback through the centuries to rest
along the fence
before moving on to meet
once more their southern foes.

A rooster crows, smoke stirs yurts.
The horses graze singly and in twos.
A shepherd astride a motorbike
herds sheep across the slope.
With no trees or rocks to tether my presence here
I walk on
toward where a dusty trail rises and disappears.

A breeze warms my back.
The rising sun devours my shadow.
The warriors are gone.
I see the white poplar posts I mistook for my ancient heroes.
Their bones I wish I could breathe back whole.

# Ghost Fortress: Yu Men Pass

Here, in the vast desert waste
where low clouds bury stars
the cold winds howl through the old fortress
guarding the ancient empire's western frontier.

We dead follow
tearing through long vanished alleys
clawing at doorless abodes
stopping in caves in which emptiness accumulates
where even the hours dare not hesitate.

At night we carve out a fresh army
of sand demons to guard
the forsaken *cheng*.[4]

Fragile, our once mortal dreams
had been but flesh for the winds to strip clean.
Bones to skeleton the dawn of day.

---

[4] fortress

## In the Forbidden Palace

The Sons of Heaven had long left.
The dynasties gone with the wind and dust.

Like a river, the endless line of tourists
meanders down gilded halls emptied now
of harried footsteps and cowered genuflection.

No echoes of intriguing voices or whispered entreats.
No golden palanquins wait for their imperial riders.

In the royal chambers dragon robes hung without wearers.
Phoenix beds made without their brocade sleepers.

No foreign convoys cross the vast marbled courtyards
enclosed by white balustrades and carved colonnades.

No tributes are borne through arched carmine gates.
In the Time pavilion, ornate clocks sit unwound.

Inside the palace of imperial treasures
jewels of jade and silver are encased behind glass.

The unbroken tide of visitors comes daily.
They gawk, admire, snap photos, take videos.

I am one, camera in hand.
Images of history captured in milliseconds
flare in an instant in my consciousness
disappear like ripples into the dim labyrinth of memory.

## Brief Reign

*— for Li Yu, poet and last ruler of Southern Tang (937–978 CE)*

Teeth of machines tear at green hills
white birch vales. The muscles of men
churn at wheat and millet fields.
Shovels and picks have no fleshly eyes
to sort precious relics.
Should they one day crack open
your subterranean tomb, what then, Prince?
Your skeleton strung, displayed
in a wooden box layered with sand
your sarcophagus glassed in
sacrificial vessels placed in wrong order
handful of corroded coins
palace bells whose ruined sounds dully echo
ceremonial gowns lain in tatters?

After the experts scrutinize, categorize
tourists visit in irreverent streams.
Guides' spiels, camera flashes
invade the last of your dark sanctity.
Few pause to read the simple lines that explain
your brief reign. Few know the depth of your loving.
Fewer still to grieve your anguished passing.
You would prefer to remain in anonymity
beneath earth's eternal sheathing.
Not to have your humiliation replayed, your afterlife
ravished again and again in the light of day.

# A Living Heritage

*—for Li Yu, poet and last ruler of Southern Tang (937–978 CE)*

In Kaifeng Palace my tourist's steps elude chains.
Eave bells beckon me down painted corridors.

Beneath these mansions
lie seven dynasties that once cradled the Middle Kingdom
their power spread and feared beyond
the Ten-Thousand Li Wall        the four seas
the Kunlun passes.

I climb the West Pavilion
the way you had done, alone at dusk
to sit and drink your favourite Three Stone wine.

You would never know your own palaces in Jinling
their sculptured hills and gardens
lie too under centuries' ruins.

How heavy your shame must have been
when your captured boat sailed into Kaifeng Fu.
Ruling Prince fallen.
Maker of songs and music silenced.
Within your strident prison walls the sound
of *wutung* leaves rubbing locked in your remorse
the cries of your beloved, keen darts.

Kingdoms that once rose
the wind and ash reclaim.
Great men of history the myths diminish.
I wish you to know, great Prince
the sorrow that flowed from your pen
moves more than your own generation of hearts.
Your poetry runs in my veins
surely as the red dust of this land.

## On Peacock Tower[5]

In the gilded censer the fragrance is cold.
The silken counterpane tosses like waves.
Rising, a heaviness in my limbs.
My hair hangs in unwashed tangles.

Dust from habit layers over my fine things.
Outside the curtains the sun has burned up half the day.

The aches inside, so much I wish to tell you.
But never mind.

This new thinness—
comes not from autumn
or from too much wine.

But never mind.

You are gone—
A thousand songs of farewell have not detained you.

Never mind.

Thinking of you on your way to distant Wuling.
The wall of smoke and mist in between.
I'm grateful for the river flowing past Peacock Tower
witnessing my watching.

Watching thus adds a new length of sorrow to the long road.

[5] A poem by Li Qing Zhao (1084–1151 CE), the author's translation.

## Ancestor Worship

My father remembers his first boat journey
with his father, uncles, clan brothers.
Two days and a night it had taken
their sampan laden with offerings,
rocking side to side as it sailed past
bamboo groves and rice paddies along the canal
past string of mud brick hovels
a Confucian temple or two.

At night they moored under a stone bridge
where he first heard of how his forebears
had been forced to abandon their ancestral homes in Fujian
flee for their lives, braving sickness and starvation
to finally settle down in marshes and the low land of the South.

At the grave mounds of their ancestors on the hill
they pulled away handfuls of grass and weeds.
Planted white silk banners that flapped in the spring breeze.
Set out their offerings: fruits, wine, a roast pig
bundles of incense, their fragrant smoke mingling
with scent of new pine and moist earth in their nostrils.
Below them, the canal and river wended
disappearing into distant valleys.

Solemn and reverent
he bowed and prayed beside his fellow clansmen
secured in their presence, in the ring of lineage and kin,
unaware of the dark shadow history portended
of the uprooting sojourn that awaited him.

# 4

## Unmarked Paths

## First Encounter

You go   without directions.
A well-trodden trail
or one unmarked, as long it's one
you have never taken before.

You know it by the absence of a sign nailed high
on an old fir or spruce along the way.

You like the surprises:
       a glimpse of hidden islets
       a snow-crowned mountain in mid-July
       the intimate way the sun filters
            through the forest canopy
       the sudden sheer drop at your feet.

One would say you like to court death
or is it love? The kind you cling to
like a sudden shimmer
and the way leads on,
you walking
holding the weight of the universe with your breath.

## In the Old Forest

The diaphanous damsel of the woods
touches my prismed heart

sings garlands of rainbows
from tip to cedar tip—

She knows mysteries
of the stars and grass.

Pirouetting in the cathedral gloom
she lets loose long-kept secrets—

The way the sun pulls taut
the butterfly's patterned flight

scattering sequined dust
the clouds carry over the mountains.

Hot breaths like chained memory:
Let me unfold my dreams here.

Echoes of singing corpse flowers
thread through the breeze.

Old-growth giants creak and sway.
There are paths ending and beginning.

All night rain prattles on green canopy.

# Footprints

Wrong turn at the end of the trail
a switchback hidden by screen of scraggy shrubs
easily missed.

Now you scramble over moss-covered logs
decayed in the damp west coast air.
Grab at clinging nettles that draw stinging

lines of blood and tears as the sun clears
the eastern ridge, its heat seeping
through the canopy warming the woods.

You follow the Baden Powell
pausing beside a large boulder that partly blocks the path
for a glimpse of the Lions through blue-grey haze.

Down to the bottom of the gully, then up
climbing higher and higher
the trail flanked by hemlocks, firs, cedars.

Exposed roots striate the trail strewn with rocks
worn slippery-smooth by snow, rain, hikers.
Sweat snakes down your neck and back.

Your city lungs strained. As the terrain grows steeper
the trail narrows. At places you have to pull yourself
up by rope and chain. Gasp for breath, snatches

of conversation on the wind dwindle then stop.
Why this stubborn need to keep going?
It comes to you as you stand weak and trembling on the West Lion.

It's in your blood, in the stories you'd heard as a child
of ancient poets and sages who travelled vast distances
through thick forests of bamboo and pine

to reach the sacred mountains on whose soaring summits
they stood humbled by their own smallness
as they gazed up at the high sky
at the endless sea of rising peaks.

# On Thin Air

The day her ex remarried she took me on
a hike up Brunswick Peak overlooking
the hazy sound, the sleepy islands.
Another summit, a different atmosphere
to reclaim herself.

All that August afternoon we laboured under
a white-torch sun, the air thin
struggling over rock-strewn clear-cuts
through fields of stiff fireweed, wilting pearly white.
Shimmering heat waves rose from the dusty ground.

My lungs screamed, gasping for breath.
I wanted to die on the spot
where the sun edged toward the chain of sapphire isles.
Not used to giving up she urged me on.

We ate our meal, peanut butter and jam sandwiches
then pushed on. A breeze blew
humming though lacy hemlocks, old pines.
The sun spilled its last gold into the copper sound.
We stood to look at the spectral moon

taunting us from high above the jagged summit.
In silence I hid the knots of my cramped muscles.
She, her five-foot-three, ninety-pound pride.

Washed by moonlight, the bare slope to the peak
changed to layer of loose shale
tearing loose under our unsure footholds
as the valley sank into night's darkness.
I stopped, waited for her to be the first to reach the top.
She froze, her hands clenched white on the final stretch.

# Hollyburn

What words hung on their lips
when they hike past us, three ancient misfits
toddling down the rock-strewn ski run in July?

One, our guide, his hair wispy, his concave chest bare
except for tufts of grey, ridged line of scarred
tissue where the doctors sawed it open.

His thighs and legs skin-wrapped bones
like those afflicted by rickets
a strange creature one might feel pity
except he could drive you mad as we hike
with his one-sided ranting
stating again and again
how unworthy the human race.

The other two, my friend and I.
She is tall and straight, her hair silver blond.
Her no-nonsense strides, crystal-grey eyes
reflect a clarity of thought, fairness.

And me, short, heavy-legged, ash-streaked hair
a wind-flung mess walking with my head bowed
thinking it has been decades since we first hiked
these mountains with our guide,
who had shown us places we'd never dreamed of.

Today, our first time out together in years
what remains of the old-growth forest
its few towering cedars and firs,
old comrades we see again with new eyes.

# Crone

I speak to the dead
spectral presences who are closer,
more real than those living, rational
beings who never show me the far side of
mortal consequences.

The dead or those who live in my memory
have acquired coral tongues—
interpret the world in cut-crystal waves
brightly showcase their prismed pain.

I speak to the unforgotten
whose lives and mine collide
as light into light leaving me
with the wisdom to let go.

In their presence time is perpetually negotiable.
I can be infant or young girl.
The woman initiated into the art of becoming.

# Seaworthy

She finds the missing jigsaw piece
meant for her to see

as she is meant to wait
while the half-completed picture

lay in its crushed cardboard box
she couldn't throw out for fear

the past would self-destruct.
Surprised at how she still recognizes

the shapes and colours.
How her fingers know

where each piece should meet—
The lighthouse flashes its white beam

across a glassy sea.
Across the indigo sky the moon flees.

Waves breaking on rocks
bring echoes of forgotten shanties.

Fine sprays wet her face.
She licks the salt from her lips

lost in the ecstasy of placing
the last piece

that fits the prow perfectly.
The boat glides over the waters

she at the oars.

## Language Lesson

The secret
of this feathery, wizened globe
bobbing in the late spring day
lies in its erect-yielding stance against the wind.

Come—
if you looked only at the underside
of clouds you would never see
the stars unfold in layers.

The first wildflowers picked in a field of knee-high grass
were the bright yellow discs     opened to the sun     its warm scent.
Had I known that away from the sun        they would close
          I would not have discarded their still-breathing corpses.

Among my collection of pressed flowers there are wild columbine
heart-leaved arnica          wintergreen.
There are no dandelions
flattened and splayed in crucified fashion.

They were the first flowers I silenced.
They are the second language I learn.
I speak it without words   like love
or the dance of stars,
the dandelions and I share,
          in the scented shadow of the sun.

# Stopping in a Cathedral in Toulon

No matter that your baptism was initiated
by colonial conquest, I cannot resist

searching every cathedral I come to
slipping into each domed dim

fragmented by shards of blood-tinged light.
The vibrant, painted portraitures

kaleidoscope of scripture tales
I know only in unsanctified segments

like other stories I carry, a desire for completion.
The arched and pillared altar, rows of white candles

flickering, wooden pews polished by holy supplication
echoes of silent prayers. I am back—

An early spring twilight, shadows of cascading rain
your pained voice, opened the wound

old as the first light in a world
newly created. It wept afresh.

Camino

At last, the steps of the cathedral—
exhausted
my face covered in sweat
my clothes dusty.

For nearly half a month I've walked
followed the footsteps of devout pilgrims
to know their ecstasy
trails tramped hard by their faith.

From Lyons to Astorga to Rabanal.
Through towns and villages
with cobbled streets and stone churches
little changed by time.

On blistered feet I trudged
over arched Romanesque bridges
though farmyards scattered with straw
chickens and goat droppings.

Climbed the rock-strewn road to Jesus's cross
Michael's shrine, festooned with celebratory ribbons
flapping in the warm breeze.
Threaded my way through hillside vineyards

groves of olive, oak, pine, eucalyptus
the hot sun redolent with astringent scents.
At night gratefully collapsed into unfamiliar beds
to ease stiff and aching muscles.

In morning rose to grey sky and impending rain
but my questing spirit refused to be dampened.
And now I climb the smooth stone steps
to the high arced doors. Breathe in frankincense

lit candles wafting from the cathedral's vaulted nave.
From the dim inside whispered prayers reverberate.
Still wondering, I pause at the threshold before entering,
then make my way to the saint's sepulchre.

# Taklamakan

The caravans had vanished.
Trails the wind and sand buried.
Silenced: the multilingual haggle
over horses, tobacco, silk, spices, tea.

We bus through high grassland where brooks
bound, sounding like tambourines, girls
dancing in bare feet, their anklet bells ringing
layers of their bright organza skirts swirling.

At night we sit around an open fire
cumin lamb roasting, yak-milk tea
sliced Xinjiang melons, sweet pomegranates
ebullient songs the children shyly sing.

For sleep we decline the fur-lined yurt.
On bed of cooling dunes we lie down
under a dark sea crowded with distant stars
witness to journeys silk traced.

The ancient caravaners appear
with tales of endless treks
from oasis outposts to bazaars and market towns
across sun-baked deserts and vast expanses

of scrub and wasteland, along icy goat trails
cut into the waists of soaring mountains
jagged cliffs covered with year-round snow.

Little did they know—
when the dust of their caravans had settled

they left behind a new world
remade in the worn image of the old.

## Primal

This old body has grown rusty, stiff. It creaks and protests
as I climb, the moon hidden. At each step my foot sinks deep

into the sliding sand. On hands and knees I half crawl to the ridge.
Gusts of cool wind tug loose my scarf. Down in our camp the dancing

has stopped. Sound of thunderous drumbeat grows faint across the valley.
Under starlight dunes dissolve. Camels hunker down

for the night. I lie on warm sand listening to the wind blow
across the desert as it has since the beginning.

The moon breaks free, full and near. It bathes the world in snowy light.
I close my eyes letting go time, senses, aware only of my own slow

breathing. In my mouth a taste of old fear going back millennia
when consciousness was first born. When humankind first pointed

at the same moon and stars and knew isolation
terrifying and trembled.

# 5

## The Way Home

# Running with Tigers

This hour our last in our ancestral home. Our belongings in light bundles: a jar of water from the village well, a packet of soil taken from the ground outside our door, a piece of red paper bearing generations of our ancestors' names as we wait on the granite threshold, edges polished by young and old calves and soles, waiting for sky to lighten.

The morning we set out for the hills, an hour's walk from home, the sky had not yet whitened. Heavy summer dew wet our hair and tunics. Night-blooming gardenia and wild orchids scented the breeze. A lone bird called from the paddies rippling in dark waves. When the sun rose over the eastern ridge we reached the valley, and began climbing. Two childhood friends, alone on the sun-splashed slope, played at gathering twigs for fuel. Frequently, we turned our eyes to the caves across the valley. The green and yellow grass in shadows, tall enough to hide the tigers. How glad we were when a farmer, a hoe over one shoulder, entered the valley.

When the Japanese soldiers occupied the villages, the dogs went about with tails between their legs. Now that the super-rich entrepreneurs in their Mercedes and Rolls-Royces, with a hunger for tiger virility have spread everywhere, will the tigers be brave enough to stay? Perhaps, like us, they will run with tatters of legends in their teeth.

## Family House

No more mud-caked footprints trail over the threshold.
No door creaks in evening or yawns open at fish-belly morning.

No baby suckles or cries or death from killing pox.
No mother weeps, no father grumbles at the thin rice gruel.

No village mender calls here for broken plow or cracked cauldron.
No junkman stops for bits of rubber, rusted iron or ox bones.

No guests come to partake in a son's wedding banquet.
No more funeral procession, no mourners, no *haidi*[6] wails.

The moon slips its yellow beams through the roof's bent ribs.
Shadows swallow the heaps of broken dishes and dirt.

The garden, a tangle of nettle, creeps the fallen walls.
Water hyacinth chokes the well where snakes now dwell.

Morning glory vines strangle the lonely acacia.
Wasps feed on papyrus whose seeds the earth ignores.

Thieves hide their loot here for pre-dawn retrieval.
Dare not ask what tragic misfortunes occurred here.

To speak of those who'd lived here is to recall long buried
memories of their sorrows and heartbreaks.

---

[6] A reed pipe, traditionally used in funeral processions.

# Things We Cannot Bring

High up in the blue-white heavens
our ears droned the unknown miles
three migratory creatures flying
mapless. No certain return.

Dark shadows under our mother's eyes
her mouth a thin line holding in
the upside-down days and years
ahead, beyond her grasp.

For two days and nights in motion
sickness, she shook her head at
the meals brought by the neutral-voiced
attendants suited in gaberdine blue.

My brother and I ate, read *Bugs Bunny*
*Woody Woodpecker* in Cantonese, slept.
Across the International Date Line, blackness
stretched on to make up the charted lost

day. Snow-caped mountains at last rose
up to meet us. The land grabbed us
thudding and bumping. Cold wind cut into
our pale mango skin as Mother gripped our hands.

Somewhere inside the labyrinth of the stark
wooden building a heavier version of our
father waited in a long brown coat, five-o'clock
shadow, twisting his grey felt hat.

*Last days*
*in our village*
*the way*
*the hills*
*the glazed tiles*
*glinted*

*In the river*
*the boys swam naked*

*Behind leafy screen*
*the girls*
*giggled*

*laughter ringing*
*rippling*
*over rice fields turning to*
*pale gold*

*Night came and sat*
*with us as*

*Po Po taught us*
*Jade Buddha chants*

*Above us*
*a trillion stars*
*blazed*

## Harvest at Lu Yang

Corn dry on asphalt rectangles
as trucks lumber past, bellowing soot.
A woman in a polyester blouse, skirt
unsteady heels, steps from her dim shop

flings a basin of water across the dirt
nearly drenching the girl riding her mangled
tricycle and a skeletal dog.
The ditch a putrescent sheen.

Red and white polyurethane bags
are heaped against a fence of dust-coated shrubs.
Beyond, migrant construction workers
labour to fill the vacated acres.

An old man leans on his bamboo cane
peering through the newly erected village gate
at the narrow road that leads to paddies
laid to waste by unprecedented droughts.

Lands forfeited by entrepreneur farmers
now sprout featureless high-rises that gird the city.
Grown fat and rich, they sit in market stalls
hawking factory-made souvenirs

to the assembly line of tourists.

# Home (1)

The endless flow of passengers deposits us
on the crowded white-tiled platform.

Whistle shrills, engine groaning
wheels creaking, the train gathers speed.

Behind us Zhengzhou's neon forest pulls away.
Ahead twin tracks thread.

Through the grimy window we see abandoned fields.
Across Huang He, its waters weaving between

high archways and silted channels.
Gongyi, an hour from Kaifeng.

At night the pale moon follows the squares
of yellow thrown from the train.

At dawn a mist unfurls.
Patchwork of millet and wheat rush past.

Handan, Baoding, Suzhou of the Jiangsu region—
The strange-sounding names slip from our tongues

with nostalgic echoes
as we enter the Pearl Delta, a jumble

of modern towns and cities glinting through clog of haze
then San Hui county, our long-awaited old home.

Nearly half a century, children who greet us
at the door ask, smiling, where we come from.

# Home (2)

Monsoon in southern Guangdong postpones
Shanghai flights. Waiting among a sea
of faces etched with resignation
numbing cold blasting from overhead a/c,
she struggles to catch the PA's garbled words.
Her shy Mandarin barely keeps her connected.

*Legend of White Snake* on her lap
she slips back to that sweltering port swollen
with coolies and post-war beggars
grimy shops, broken streets,
and the old hotel they stayed in
on their way to the Lo Wu border
the hard plank beds crawling with bugs...

Guangzhou: her eyes open wide
at forests of modern office high-rises
row upon row of charmless apartment buildings
as the bus navigates the city's rush hour traffic.
Rivers of vehicles foreign and local made
lap along concrete highways, loop and criss-cross

into densely packed suburbs
that replace vanishing villages and fields.
Past factories and warehouses in the falling dusk
she strains for a glimpse of green paddies dimly rippling.
At last a hopeful line of grey brick dwellings half hidden
behind a dripping stand of willows.

She enters the crimson arched gate guarded
by clay idols that serve as benevolent gods resurrected.
Beyond, no scent of straw-fire smoke
no sound of children at twilight play.
The lane zigzags through the village's
newly erected houses, white-tiled, forbidding.

# North Pacific

The cannery stands wordless and apologetic
in a coat of glossy white paint.
The new cedar boardwalk strings together
the former salt house, reduction plant
cookhouse, company store, the manager's
and the foreman's houses—
all resurrected from near-ruins—

are not the things I've come to see.

Nor the river that flows past under a grey mist
or the mountains rising from its steep shores.
Not the ghosts of men and women
who once worked here, the long-vanished
fishing boats, the noisy gulls.

I've come in remembrance
of the community once knitted from threads
of multi-textured voices
each one singing of their dreams stolen, erased
by crushing winds of this fragile land.

Women and men who came together
each summer, alone or with family, to labour—sweat
as storms gathered in lakes and mountains.
The rivers yielded their last bounties of salmon.

The winds have calmed. I take my leave
carry in my heart echoes of those silenced voices
of all that has been lost.

# Heron, Stone Shadow

On legs of stilts you stalk the curved shore
wearing your twilight blue coat,
head held still, listening.

We are both returning sojourners,
though your presence here
has preceded mine: necessity over desire.
Survival against memory's tremor.
How complete your simplicity, your immunity.

I sit half hidden in the tall grass.
In the morning light the river's gentle waves
shimmer like fragments of cerulean glass.
The thought tossing wind of other Augusts invades.
You step further up the shallows, pause,
still as a stone shadow.

A morning as calm as this, the hills on Smith Island
nestling deep in the river's reclaimed bed—
Hemlocks and firs line the slopes patching
and repatching the fire-bared places, crowding out
the branched skeletons picked white by the near
year-around rain.

The mist ascends at the junction where the slough
curves away from the Skeena flowing in its ponderous way
to the ocean from where the sockeye and coho once returned.

You were not here then.
Eons of evolutionary instinct had warned you to stay away
from the chugging boats, the effluvium, the profusion of diesel
and oil waste, profaning your sanctuary.

A roar of a boat's motor in the distance—
Untroubled, you lift your sword-slender beak.
A flash of silver in between, a prize for your patience.

Strangers we are. It's what keeps us aware.

## Lamplight, Window Boxes

Silence wakes me to the night.
I am alone in the cabin that smells of mildew.
The blankets are heavy from the tenacious damp.

The air invades with unseasoned chill.
Outside, the dripping rain tells me
I am back.

Down the boardwalk the row of bright yellow lamps
stand like beacons, beckoning the fleet of seine boats
and trawlers now long gone.

I sit down on a sodden plastic chair outside the mess hall.
They had not salvaged the beautiful window boxes
my father, the cannery cook, had made.

How the profusion of lobelia,
pansy and nasturtium he planted each summer
had brought the hummingbirds, butterflies and bees.

Inside the dimly lit cannery museum are sepia photos,
maps, rusted tools, a hodgepodge of fishing
equipment and canning machines,

a few workers' biographical compilations, incomplete.
The loft where the women worked for sixty-cents-an-hour wage
is now a storage for items whose histories

no one cares to look into, like my father's flower boxes
and his dovetailed cabinet. The carpenter told me
he wanted to cry when he sawed them to pieces.

# Footfalls

My footprints behind yours
through eye of the needle
daughter to mother to daughter
to son,
the steps I take
reverberating across centuries.
The way encoded.

Our lives concentric rings
growing outward, lilies and roses nourished
by sun and rain, the dark earth.

We walk in shadow, our steps grow firmer
our footfalls louder, thunder
across teeming valleys, deserts
echo through colonnaded halls and chambers.

In our bellies we carry the fire
that fuelled our forebears onward.
In our veins, a river of stories and memories
illuminates our ancient paths.

# Oceans

Swollen with autumn rain the brook
splashes and gurgles below the footbridge
where we drop our flaming leaves
dash to the other side to watch

our leaf boats come twisting
somersaulting, swirling around snags
half-submerged boulders.
More leaves we set sailing, laughing.

Two years old—
the answers to all the questions you will ask
are in the bright blue sky

the yellowing grass, the quickening wind
the towering cypress, roosting crows
and the brook that flows on
commingling with oceans.

Answers you will instinctually know.

Your small hand I hold to begin our journey home.
On other journeys you won't need me.
Of all the possible meetings—collisions
our paths cross but briefly.

## Joy of Flying

The mind retreats,
shrinks to a green plum pit.
Thoughts sink
pulled by centrifugal weight,
the dull throbbing criss-crossing the brain.

There are times when it rises
out of its corporeal cage, trailing its sensed
cache across time and space,
blazing in coral-ringed symphonies.

*We meet on the north bank of the Yangtze.*
*The moon is like a hook.*
*The breeze has vacated the painted pavilion.*
*Your peipa lies unstrummed.*
*Where is she who fills your cup with hinted grace?*
*In her absence the grass grows long.*

I don't know whose lines are these.
I am rising, rising to the moon's crystalline hook.

## Acknowledgements

With special thanks to the editors of the following journals in which a number of these poems, some in slightly different form, first appeared:

*PRISM international*: "Bones and Seeds," "Lotus Girl," and "On Peacock Tower."

*Grain*: "Bears of Yan An," "Harvest at Lu Yang," "Dawn: Inner Mongolia," "Taklamakan," and "Ghost Fortress: Yu Men Pass." They are from a suite of poems, "China Sojourn: 2011," that took third place in the 2013 Short *Grain* Contest.

*Ricepaper*: "Brief Reign," "Things We Cannot Bring," "Lamplight, Window Boxes."

"On Thin Air" took second place at the Burnaby Writers' Society Annual Writing Contest in 2013. "Language Lesson" took first place in the Burnaby Writers' Society Annual Writing Contest in 2003.

My deep gratitude to:

The Canada Council for the Arts for its financial assistance.

Publisher Karen Haughian for giving me the opportunity to have my work published with Signature Editions and to Clarise Foster for her insightful and skillful editing.

The Writer's Studio at Simon Fraser University for providing me with the rare opportunity to learn and to grow as a writer.

Jen Currin, our mentor at The Writer's Studio (2012) at Simon Fraser University and my fellow cohorts for their support and friendships.

I am indebted to poet mentor Jami Macarty for her expertise, her sure eye and ear, and to poets Evelyn Lau and Fiona Tinwei Lam for their kind encouragement and support.

A special thank you to my family for their patience throughout the years.

## About the Author

Caroline Wong, a graduate of the Simon Fraser University Writer's Studio, is a writer of fiction and poetry. Her short stories have been published in *Ricepaper, Canadian Tales of the Fantastic* and *Winners' Circle Nine.* Her poetry has appeared in *Grain, PRISM international, The Prose-Poem Project, Ricepaper* and *West Coast Line.* A suite of poems, "China Sojourns: 2011," took third place in the 2013 Short *Grain* Contest.

In 2014, with a travel and research grant from the Canada Council for the Arts, she returned to her ancestral home in southern China to interview her aging aunt, the only remaining family member who knew the family history. The trip allowed her to spend time with her aunt and numerous cousins, whom she had briefly visited only twice before since she immigrated to Canada as a young girl.

Eco-Audit
Printing this book using Rolland Enviro100 Book
instead of virgin fibres paper saved the following resources:

| Trees | Electricity | Water | Air Emissions |
|-------|-------------|-------|---------------|
| 2 | 3GJ | 1m³ | 108kg |